God's
REVIVING
PRESENCE

Offspring PUBLISHERS

www.offspringpublishers.com

ISBN 978-0-9838105-9-9

First Printing 2012

Printed in the United States of America

Copyright © 2012 by David Ravenhill

Includes: All editorial, revisions including cover design, page layout and formatting.

All rights reserved. No portion of this book may be reproduced in any form without the written permission of the author.

Book design by Lorinda Gray/Ragamuffin Creative
www.ragamuffincreative.com

God's REVIVING PRESENCE

JAMES ALEXANDER STEWART

Formerly titled: *Revival and You*

Foreword by David Ravenhill

About the Author

Part of my father's legacy was his library which now surrounds the walls of my office, some four thousand book or more. Among the many volumes are books by John Wesley, Charles Finney, A. W. Tozer, Andrew Murray, Charles Spurgeon, G. Campbell Morgan and a host of other well know authors, preachers and teachers.

A lesser known name may be that of James Alexander Stewart, the author of this book (formerly titled *Revival and You*). James Alexander Stewart began his evangelistic ministry as a lad of 14 years of age in his native Glasgow, Scotland. For 44 years he travelled as an evangelist in different parts of the world. He preached in every country of Europe except Albania.

Along with his wife, he wrote almost 60 books and booklets, many of which have been translated into other languages. His burden was to see a mighty outpouring of the Spirit of God sweep through the Church in revival fire. He lived to see this burden come true in many places.

This book sets forth in a fervent and practical manner the pathway to Revival. Out of a wealth of experience, the author takes the reader by the hand and leads them along the pathway to blessing. The late Richard Wurmbrand said, "James Stewart was the last foreign preacher to evangelize my country of Rumania. I was one of his last interpreters and I saw God work in an extraordinary way in Revival throughout my country. I could never forget the sermons he preached. They inspired and encouraged me during my years of imprisonment."

Professor Ferenc Kiss wrote, "Not since the Reformation days did my country receive such revival blessing as under James Stewart's ministry."

Revivalists are rare today, especially in the Western World. While many claim the title, few deliver the goods. James A. Stewart was one of those rare individuals who spoke and wrote from experience. As my father repeatedly said to me growing up, "A man with an experience is never at the mercy of a man with an argument." Revival happened and can happen again. Read how!

—David Ravenhill

Table of Contents

Foreword 7

Introduction 8

Chapter 1   The Promise of Revival 11

Chapter 2   Prayer Which Brings Revival 21

Chapter 3   The Local Church, the Centre of Revival 35

Chapter 4   Worldliness and Revival 53

Chapter 5   The Holy Spirit and Revival 63

Chapter 6   Satan's Great Snare in Times of Revival 77

Chapter 7   An Urgent Appeal 85

Foreword

James Stewart and I have been friends and prayer partners for many years. I have, I believe, every one of his books and booklets. To really evaluate the vitality of his writings would take literally pages. As I have read the new book, twice over, it is my prayerful conviction that the chapter-headings alone, if prayed over, could start Revival.

Again, and among other things, this book will be a source-book for sermon outlines and illustrations for all Christian workers in preparing for revival.

The author knows what he is talking about as he has had the privilege of seeing God work in mighty revivals in Europe. He has also been blessed in a singular way in his meetings on the North American continent. In some places where I have been, I have discovered he has become a legend.

I pray that God will bless this book mightily.

—Hyman Appelman

James Alexander Stewart

Introduction

The modern day Church lies lifeless and in a deep self induced coma, unaware of her true spiritual condition. Never has she needed a true touch of God more than today. Her vital signs are barely visible and the end is imminent. Apart from the sovereign intervention of Almighty God we will not make it.

What has happened to the Church that has brought about such a dismal ending to such a glorious beginning. Called and chosen as His bride, we have instead lusted after every carnal, despicable, degrading, worldly pleasure imaginable. Gone is our appetite for the things of God; replaced instead is our love for the world. We have chosen to defile our garments and dress and act like the world around us rather than preparing for the return of our great and glorious Bridegroom.

The early Church turned the world upside down. The modern Church has allowed the world to turn her upside down. First called Christians at Antioch because of their close resemblance to Christ, today we are no longer recognized as acting anything like Him. We have chosen instead to blend in with society and hide our light under a bushel. Truly our salt has lost its flavor. We have become lethargic, lazy, lukewarm and blind to our own condition.

It's time to lay aside all the Madison Avenue ways and turn in desperation to the very source of life Himself. Our worldly ways have produced nothing of lasting value. Our "seeker sensitive churches" have instead turned out to be insensitive, insipid, and unresponsive congregations that relish the message of self improvement, but shun any mention of sin and sanctification.

The only remedy is revival. We have sought satisfaction from cisterns that hold no water and refused to drink from the living water that only God can give.

This little book you are holding is full of examples showing the difference that God can make if we truly seek Him with all our heart. It's not too late. We may closely resemble the Laodicean Church, but remember that Jesus addressed them with sternness and yet hope when he stated, "Those whom I love I reprove, and discipline…"

Read this book on your knees. Open your heart afresh to God and allow Him to touch and revive your life with His presence. I know He will. It's His longing. Is it yours?

— David Ravenhill
November 2012

CHAPTER 1

The Promise of Revival

"Search and see, look in the Book and read; was there any who did trust Him that was put to shame!"

—JOHN BUNYAN

"A few souls in any church or school or mission field may inaugurate a new condition by praying through and standing on the promises of God."

—J. A. S.

"*Search and see,*" *exclaims Bunyan.* "Look in the Book and read; was there any who did trust in Him that was put to shame!"

How often I have been inspired and helped during times of persecution and discouragement in the mission field by the bright promises of Jehovah!

"A man shall be as an hiding-place from the wind, and a covert from the tempest; as rivers of waters in a dry place, as the shadow of a great rock in a weary land" (Isa. 32:2).

"The Lord shall command the blessing upon thee in thy storehouses, and in all that thou settest thine hand unto; and He shall bless thee in the Land which the Lord thy God giveth thee" (Deut. 28:8).

"Fear ye not, stand still, and see the salvation of the Lord, which He will show to you today; for the Egyptians whom ye have seen today, ye shall see them again no more forever. The Lord shall fight for you, and ye shall hold your peace" (Exod. 14:13, 14).

"One man of you shall chase a thousand; for the Lord your God, He it is that fighteth for you, as He hath promised you" (Joshua 23:10).

"Sanctify yourselves, for tomorrow the Lord will do wonders among you" (Joshua 3:5).

"Sit still, my daughter, until thou know how the matter will fall; for the man (our Kinsman Redeemer) will not be in rest until He have finished the thing this day" (Ruth 3:18).

"For in the time of trouble, he shall hide me in his pavilion: in the secret of His tabernacle shall He hide me; He shall set me up upon a rock. And now shall mine head be lifted up above mine enemies round about me: therefore, will I offer in His tabernacle sacrifices of joy; I will sing, yea, I will sing praises unto the Lord" (Ps. 27:5, 6).

"I am the Lord thy God, which brought thee out of the land of Egypt; open thy mouth wide, and I will fill it" (Ps. 81:10).

"And the Lord shall guide thee continually, and satisfy thy soul in drought, and make fat thy bones, and thou shalt be like a watered garden, and like a spring of water whose waters fail not, and they that shall be of thee shall build the old waste places: thou shalt raise up the foundations of many generations; and thou shalt be called the repairer of the breach, the restorer of paths do dwell in" (Isa. 58:11, 12).

"No weapon that is formed against thee shall prosper; and every tongue that shall rise against thee in judgment, thou shalt condemn. This is the heritage of the servants of the Lord..." (Isa. 54:17).

"I will go before thee, and make the crooked places straight: I will break in pieces the gates of brass, and cut in sunder the bars of iron: and I will give thee the treasures of darkness, and hidden riches of secret places, that thou mayest know that I, the Lord, which call thee by thy name, am the God of Israel" (Isa. 45:2, 3).

"And I will bring the blind by a way that they knew not; I will lead them in paths that they have not known: I will make darkness light before them, and crooked things straight. These things will I do unto them, and not forsake them" (Isa. 42:16).

"The Lord thy God in the midst of thee is mighty; He will save, He will rejoice over thee with joy; He will rest in His love, He will joy over thee with singing" (Lit. Heb. "rest silently over thee in love," Zeph. 3:17).

These and a host of other promises have been claimed by martyrs, prisoners, lonely discouraged believers, and weary missionaries all down the ages when they felt their feet slipping. What stories and songs have been written concerning the faithfulness of our covenant-keeping God.

Millions of believers can testify with Moses: "There was not one city too strong for us: the Lord our God delivered all unto us" (Deut. 2:36).

Hudson Taylor, meditating on Ezekiel 34:26, "And I will make them, and the places round about My hill, a blessing; and I will cause the shower to come down in his season; there shall be showers of blessings," embraced this promise. God spoke to him through this verse, and on this text alone he predicted that God was going to do "a new thing," and he believed the Lord for the first one hundred missionaries.

James Caughey pleaded and prayed and prophesied mighty local revivals throughout England on the strength of Mark 11:24. When he arrived on the shores of Great Britain from America he quietly told evangelical Methodist leaders that God was going to do mighty things. Wherever he went he preached first on this verse, "Therefore, I say unto you, What things soever ye desire, when ye pray, believe that ye receive them, and ye shall have them." Churches were revolutionised, and tens of thousands of souls were sanctified among whom was William Booth, the founder of the Salvation Army. Said Caughey, "Mark 11:24 is a rich mine. What precious metal may be dug from it in experience! It may be likened to a magazine also; for it has furnished me much material of war."

Pastor Harms, of Hermannsberg, Germany, when appointed to his pastorate, felt discouraged because it seemed an impossible task given him. The church in the village was small and the testimony weak. His parish, ten miles square, was overgrown with unbelief and formalism. There was no concern among the unsaved.

The Promise of Revival

But as he fasted and prayed he received a mighty enduement of the Spirit, whereby he was able to receive definite promises from God's word; definite passages of Scripture which revealed to him that the whole neighbourhood would be transformed. With a little band of believers he prayed through on these promises, and very soon the desert began to blossom like a rose. Large numbers flocked to hear the Word. No year passed without new awakenings. Thousands were brought into fellowship with the Church, and so great was their depths of spirituality; and so great was their missionary spirit, that it has been said by deep mature spiritual minds that very few evangelical churches in any part of the world could equal the village church of Hermannsberg.

Jonathan Goforth, after fifteen years in China, came to the deep and painful conviction that God had something mightier to do in his life and ministry. He became restless, as he began under the Spirit's anointing an intense study of the Scriptures in relation to revival. "Every passage that had any bearing upon the price of, or the road to, the accession of power became life and breath to me," he said. After months of closet-study, he believed that God would fulfil His Word in this most difficult of mission fields. Later, at one place in Manchuria, where the Holy Spirit had descended in unusual power upon the people, the Chinese evangelist asked the missionary why he had not told them that there was going to be revival. The missionary, in deep humiliation, replied that he, himself, up to a time ago, had not known that such was possible.

The story of the Telegue Mission in India is a thrilling one. The Canadian Baptist Missionary Society had only one station, right away by itself, and so it was called "The Lone Star Mission." The missionary who laboured there found himself alone because of a shortage of workers, and it was resolved by the Mission Board that instead of giving him a helper they would close down the station. Boldly and bluntly the missionary told the Board that he would carry on alone, if only to leave his bones there as a witness to Christ. Touched by his impassioned earnestness, the Board resolved to make one more attempt, and a helper was sent. The lonely labourers definitely claimed and believed, on the authority of the Word of God, that a mighty movement of the Spirit was coming. Before long their prayers were answered, and the good news was flashed back to the thousands of praying saints in North America that God had performed a miracle. As strong an authority as Dr. A. T. Pierson has left on record: "Probably the largest number of people baptised at one time since the Day of Pentecost took place at the Lone Star Mission. Two thousand two hundred and twenty-two converts were baptised in a single day!"

For seven years **Adoniram Judson** sought the conversion of the Burmese, and when advised by the Missionary Society to surrender his mission and start in another field he answered, "No! No! I cannot and will not surrender this mission. Success is as certain here as the promise of a faithful God can make it." Then came the Burmese blessing.

Henry Martyn once wrote: "How shall it ever be possible to convince a Hindu or a Brahmin of anything?…Truly, if ever I see a Hindu a real believer in the Lord Jesus I shall see something more nearly approaching the resurrection of a dead body than anything I have yet seen." But Martyn carried on in faith, believing the promises of God, and lived to see the day when God worked just this miracle among the heathen.

As I myself have waited before the Lord, I have received definite promises of revival, for different churches and different countries. The result has been a mighty quickening among the saints and the salvation of thousands of souls. Such promises given to me have been:

"Behold, I will do a new thing; now it shall spring forth; shall ye not know it? I will even make a way in the wilderness, and rivers in the desert" (Isa. 43:19).

"Thou shalt be a blessing…I will bless thee…" (Gen. 12:2).

"Sanctify yourselves, for tomorrow the Lord will do wonders among you" (Joshua 3:5).

"Behold, I will make thee a new sharp threshing instrument, having teeth: thou shalt thresh the mountains, and beat them small, and shall make the hills as chaff…when the poor and needy seek water and there is none, and their tongue faileth for thirst, I the Lord will hear them, I the God of Israel will not forsake them. I will open rivers in high places and fountains in the midst of the valleys: I will make the wilderness a pool of water, and the dry land springs of water" (Isa. 41:15-18).

"Call unto me and I will answer thee, and show thee great and mighty things, which thou knowest not" (Jer. 33:3).

"Behold, I am the Lord, the God of all flesh: is there anything too hard for Me?" (Jer. 32:27).

"The people that do know their God shall be strong and do exploits" (Dan. 11:32).

"Said I not unto thee, that if thou wouldst believe, thou shouldst see the glory of God" (John 11:40).

"And I will restore to you the years that the locust hath eaten...and ye shall eat in plenty and be satisfied, and praise the name of the Lord, your God, that hath dealt wondrously with you, and my people shall never be ashamed. And ye shall know that I am in the midst of Israel, and that I am the Lord your God, and none else; and My people shall never be ashamed" (Joel 2:25-27).

"And I will sanctify My great name, which was profaned among the heathen, which ye have profaned in the midst of them; and the heathen shall know that I am the Lord, saith the Lord God, when I shall be sanctified in you before their eyes" (Ezek. 36:23).

"For verily I say unto you, that whosoever shall say unto this mountain, be thou removed, and be thou cast into the sea; and shall not doubt in his heart, but shall believe that those things which he saith shall come to pass, he shall have whatsoever he saith" (Mark. 11:23).

"In the last day, that great day of the feast, Jesus stood and cried, saying, If any man thirst, let him come unto Me and drink. He that believeth on Me, as the Scripture hath said, out of his belly shall flow rivers of living waters" (John. 7:37, 38).

"From this day will I bless you" (Hag. 2:19).

A few souls in any church or school or mission field may inaugurate a new condition by praying through and standing on the promises of God. My brother, my sister, if the Lord has laid it on your heart to pray for revival in your sphere of labour, go alone on your knees with the Word before God. Make sure the desire is from the Lord, so that the motive will be for the glory of His dear Name, (see Daniel's prayer, Dan. 9:17-19). Then ask Him to seal to your heart some portion of His Word, according to that which He desires to do in your midst. Once you have obtained such a promise, stand on it unflinchingly until the answer comes.

> *"There shall be showers of blessing:*
> *This is the promise of love;*
> *There shall be seasons refreshing,*
> *Sent from the Saviour above.*
>
> *There shall be showers of blessing—*
> *Precious reviving again;*
> *Over the hills and the valleys*
> *Sound of abundance of rain.*
>
> *There shall be showers of blessing;*
> *Send them upon us, O Lord.*
> *Grant to us now a refreshing;*
> *Come, and now honour Thy Word.*
>
> *There shall be showers of blessing;*
> *If we but trust and obey.*
> *There shall be seasons refreshing,*
> *If we let God have His way."*
>
> —EL NATHAN

CHAPTER 2

Prayer Which Brings Revival

"If every true pastor, evangelist, and missionary throughout the world would simultaneously turn unto God in utter self-humbling, in intercession, in seeking the face of God and in repentance, such an upheaval of holy prayer would shake the world."

—D M. PANTON

"The need of the hour is for intercessors in vital union with their ascended Lord, to agonize inside the veil for deliverance of the church from its spiritual slump."

—J. A. S.

The need of the hour is for definite, prevailing, agonizing prayer for God to rend the heavens and visit His blood-bought people. Dr. R. A. Torrey has stated, "Doubtless one of the great secrets of the unsatisfactoriness and superficiality and unreality of many of our modern so-called 'revivals' is that more dependence is put upon man's machinery rather than upon God's power, sought and obtained by earnest, persistent, believing prayer." We live in a day characterized by the multiplication of man's machinery and the diminution of God's power. The great cry of our day is "Work, work, work! New organizations, new methods, new machinery." The great need of our days is prayer. It was a masterstroke of the devil when he got the Church to generally lay aside this mighty weapon of prayer. The devil is perfectly willing the Church should multiply its organization, and deftly-contrived machinery for the conquest of the world for Christ, if it will only give up praying.

Whenever you see revival in any place, if you will inquire among the members of the church or churches you will find that an unknown Jacob has been wrestling in prayer for the blessing; some Elijah, alone perhaps, with head bowed between his knees, has been praying for a spiritual deluge, and keeping a sharp look-out for the gathering clouds. The Lord cried through Ezekiel in his day, "And I sought for a man among them, that should make up the hedge, and stand in the gap before me for the land…but found none" (Ezek. 22:30). And in our day the cry is the same; *there is a great need for more intercessors in vital union with their ascended Lord, who will agonize inside the veil for the deliverance of the Church from its spiritual "slump."*

In Acts 12:5 we read that "prayer was made without ceasing of the church unto God" for Peter in prison. The word translated "without ceasing" literally means "stretched-outedly," suggesting the intensity with which the church stretched out toward God in agonizing desire for Peter's deliverance. Here we have a picture of spiritual travail among the saints for the deliverance of a brother. This is the kind of prayer that prevails with God, and brings forth response that amazes even those who are praying! Much of our modern prayers have no power in them because there is no heart in them. They lack intenseness and fervour.

True prayer is an aggressive, unseen, closet-ministry in cooperation with the Holy Spirit, for the purpose of dislodging the powers of darkness from the strategic position which they occupy in the Church and in the world. This kind of prayer brings God into the battle. "For the weapons which I wield," says Paul,…are mighty in the strength of God to overthrow the strongholds of the adversaries" (2 Cor. 10:4, Conybeare). Prayer is the Christian's secret weapon. The clarion call is for believers everywhere to "stand in the gap" and, linked with the triumphant Christ through the victory of Calvary, to bring to bear an aggressive warfare against the satanic forces.

The demons of hell are real, and Satan, the great arch-enemy of the Church, is seeking to "wear out the saints." We must recognize that it is Satan who has blinded the minds of the saints and kept them in ignorance of their birthright privileges and of their responsibility to live an overcoming life by the power of the Holy Spirit. It is he who, through worldliness, has caused them to leave their first love. It is he who seeks to hinder revival among the saints of God today. Therefore, as we pray for revival, we must not only resist our foe in the all-conquering name of the Lord Jesus, but we must proceed to drive him off the field through that same glorious Name. This we have been given the power to do through Him who "disarmed the principalities and the powers which fought against Him and put them to open shame, leading them captive in the triumphs of Christ" (Col. 2:14, Conybeare).

The early Church knew the secret of overcoming through this glorious weapon of prayer. As wave after wave of satanic opposition broke over them, they conquered on their knees. They went forward on their knees. They lived at the Throne. The need in the Church today is to rediscover the secret of power to wrestle with God like Paul and the spirit to agonize in prayer like Epaphras. Then, through our union with Christ on the Cross, prayer will be filled with the Spirit of conquest through which we will be able to vanquish the foe and shout the victory over him. It is not enough that we "resist the devil," who seeks to deceive and to divide the saints of the Lord, thus bringing impotence upon a subnormal church. The Word of God teaches us that we must be "more than conquerors" in the conquest.

"Whatsoever thou shalt bind on earth shall be bound in heaven: and whatsoever thou shalt loose on earth shall be loosed in heaven" (Matt. 16:19).

"Elias was a man subject to like passions as we are, and he prayed earnestly that it might not rain: and it rained not on the earth by the space of three years and six months. And he prayed again: and the heaven gave rain" (Jas. 5:17-18).

"Through Thee will we push down our enemies: in Thy name will we tread them under that rise up against us" (Ps. 44:5).

"How can one enter into a strong man's house and spoil his goods, except he first bind the strong man? And then he will spoil his house" (Matt. 12:29).

"I will rebuke the devourer for your sakes, and he shall not destroy" (Mal. 3:11).

Ephesians 6 portrays to us the battle arena with the battle drawn, and no quarter given to the enemy. In verses 12, 13 and 18 we read,

> Ours is not a conflict with mere flesh and blood, but with the despotisms, the empires, the forces that control and govern this dark world—the spiritual hosts of evil arrayed against us in the heavenly warfare. Therefore put on the complete armour of God, so that you may be able to stand your ground on the day of battle, and, having fought to the end, to remain victors on the field…Pray with unceasing (unwearied) prayer and entreaty on every fitting occasion in the Spirit, and be always on the alert to seize opportunities for doing so, with unwearied persistence and entreaty on behalf of all God's people (Weymouth).

The victorious intercessor, having vanquished the foe on the battlefield, must remain standing for further conquests, using the shield of faith, and wielding the sword of the Spirit. The prayer warrior goes on conquering and to conquer, standing on the ground of Christ's victory.

In the Authorized Version the admonition "watching thereunto" literally means "being sleepless thereunto." The intercessor must be alert and keep alert. He is persistent in earnest, unceasing intercession for the saints. Paul beseeches the saints in Rome to "strive" together with him in prayer. The word "strive" means primarily to contend as a warrior in a fight. The same thought is brought out in the mighty ministry of Epaphras: "Who is ever contending on your behalf in his prayers" (Col. 4:12, Conybeare). Such earnestness in prayer is illustrated graphically for us in the Garden of Gethsemane where our blessed Lord "sweat great drops of blood" (Luke 22:44). We are told that our Saviour was in great agony and "STILL He prayed more earnestly." Oh, how cold and indifferent are our own prayers in comparison! Our Lord, in the Parable of Importunity, in Luke 11:8, teaches us the same lesson of persistent, earnest asking. "Yet, because of his importunity he will arise and give him as many as he needeth." The word translated "importunity" is a very striking one, used only here in the New Testament. It means literally "barefacedness" or "shamelessness." The man of the parable was shameless in the boldness of his asking. He was shameless in awakening his neighbour at the midnight hour. He was shameless because he was desperate in his plight; he had no bread to set before his guest!

I have discovered in my own revival ministry that God only answers the prayers of the saints who are desperate. How many are praying for revival who are not burdened and broken? Hannah is set forth in the Word as a desperate believer praying for revival (1 Sam. 1). Nothing mattered in her life but that God would answer her prayer and give her a son. She was a heart-broken woman. So great was her agony that she could not speak, but could only weep. Even the high priest of God misunderstood her condition and thought she was drunk, as she went into the house of God to agonize. Hear the words of the burdened saint: "No, my Lord, I am a woman of a sorrowful spirit: I have drunk neither wine nor strong drink but have poured out my soul before the Lord" (v. 16). The reason why we have so few revivals is that we have so few desperate believers who are willing to pay the price of this closet ministry.

Mr. Finney tells of a poor consumptive who was unable to do anything more than pray. Yet so mighty was he in intercession that revivals sprang up as if spontaneously and unaccountably. After his death his diary revealed the secret behind these great blessings.

John Knox was a man so famous for his power in prayer that Queen Mary used to say that she feared his prayers more than all the mighty armies in Europe. He was often in such agony for the deliverance of his country that he could not sleep. "Lord, give me Scotland, or I die" was the cry constantly on the lips of the Reformer. So mightily did God hear his cry that "The Land of the Heather" became the most fruitful vineyard in the entire world.

The good **John Welsh** of Ayr felt that his day was ill-spent if he did not spend a t least seven or eight hours in prayers. On going to rest, he used to lay a plaid on top of the bed-clothes so that when he arose for his night prayers he might cover himself in the cold room. Sometimes he would retire to the church, which was a little distance from the town, and there pray all the night through.

One of the heart-touching incidents of Scottish history is the glorious closet-work of **William C. Burns**. He prayed for hours daily as he began his public ministry at the age of twenty. One morning, when his mother came to his bedroom to call him to his breakfast, she found him lying on the floor where he had been detained by the Spirit all night in mighty pleadings. He greeted her with the words, "Mother, God has given me Scotland today!" In a short time the whole of Scotland was shaken by a mighty spiritual upheaval without any organized effort.

In Newport, Wales, there was a prayer circle of praying men who met together every Saturday night for over thirty years to pray for blessing. Not one death occurred in the circle during this time. They began to pray, in the first place, because they felt burdened that Charles Spurgeon needed a mighty anointing as he was beginning his ministry in London. It is very remarkable to notice that on the very Lord's day following the first prayer meeting Spurgeon began to preach with such increased unction that it was noticeable to all.

To our sorrow, we have discovered many pastors and churches praying for the revival who will never see the answer to their prayers, because their church is not geared to the scriptural pattern of revival. Their programme is not that of the Spirit. There is no preparation for revival. There is no mighty upsurge of intercession. They are evangelical and orthodox. They live a quiet, consistent Christian testimony, but something is sadly lacking. There is no desperation over the sinful conditions of a sub-normal church. They know nothing of vital intercession, such as characterized the life of Elijah, whose "energized prayer was of great force."

Many times I have gone to a fine church for meetings, only to discover that, although the members loved the Lord and His Word, there was no sign of revival. There were no souls being saved. There was no outreaching to the ends of the earth with a deep foreign-mission enterprise. The reason was not far to seek. These people did not know the joy of holy travail on behalf of a sleeping Church and dying world. They spent many hours studying their Bibles, but spent very little time at the Throne. I found that there were no moral sins that kept back the blessing. It was the coldness and complacency of their own hearts. They sat at ease in Zion, with no passion for souls. When the Spirit broke them down, and filled their hearts with the fire of Christ's love, and poured out upon them the spirit of agony and intercession for the salvation of those about them, then revival came into their midst. Oh, how alarming is the condition of the evangelical Church today! How few churches have one real, desperate prayer meeting a week. We oftentimes sing, "A little talk with Jesus makes it quite all right," but, beloved, it is going to take more than a little talk with Jesus to bring revival. If, as our Lord said, it takes extraordinary prayer and fasting to cast out one demon from one person, how much less can we expect to have him cast out of the Church and the world without any?

During "The Great Awakening," Jonathan Edwards wrote with great logic:

> Why should it be thought strange that those who are full of the Spirit of Christ should be proportionately in their souls like to Christ,

who had so strong a love for them and concern for them as to be willing to drink the dregs of the cup of God's fury for them; and at the same time, as their High Priest, offer up strong crying and tears with extreme agony when He was in travail for their souls? The spirit of those that have been in distress for the souls of others in this revival, so far as I can discern, seems not to be different from that of the apostle, who travailed for souls, and was ready to wish himself accursed from Christ for others.

There has never been a true awakening anywhere on earth until there was a desperate Church. It is when we are in desperation that God steps in and answers our prayers mightily. I knew a business man, a wealthy, influential manufacturer, who was so burdened for the spiritual condition of his country that he arose every morning at five o'clock to seek the face of the Lord for this matter. For years he prayed on in faith until the answer came. He prayed that God would raise up other believers with like minds to join him all over the land in this secret ministry. So desperate was he that he told the Lord that if he would send revival, he would spend his entire wealth for the evangelization of the nation. This dear brother kept his word, as he became the human centre of the revival movement in his land.

I knew a local church in an Eastern European land which, because of coldness, had only some twenty believers gathering on Sunday night for Bible study. Some suggested that they close the building and give up their testimony in that predominantly Roman Catholic city. A few held on in faith and, with careful deliberation, being elderly people, had a solemn meeting of dedication where they told God that whatever should be the price for an awakening in their church and city they were willing to pay it. After bringing all their tithes into God's storehouse, and laying themselves on their altar, they continued for many months seeking the face of the Lord. It was the biggest thing in their life. It was the one thing that crowded their horizons. It was the theme of their talk at all times. They were brothers and sisters with a purpose. They would not let go of the Lord until He had blessed them.

When I began meetings in their church, many hundreds of souls were saved from the opening nights, many among them being the children of those who had been praying. So mightily did the Lord work in the church to the salvation of souls that very soon the building which seated some eight hundred people was packed to capacity at every meeting. Without any pastor, they soon overflowed their banks, so that some twenty mission stations were established in Roman Catholic districts around them. This place became the mother church to many groups of believers. From this church the members went forth all over their country evangelizing. The deadest church in the nation became the most spiritual and wide-awake. When the Spirit of God began to work at the beginning, so great was the power of Jehovah that they carried on meetings every night for many months. These meetings were necessary because of the power of the Spirit resting upon the young converts, who in turn were winning others for the Lord. The elderly saints who had waited before the Lord now had the joy of building up the young converts in the most holy faith.

In another country in Europe, when a bishop thanked me for the revival which had taken place in his denomination during the course of several years, in which his own life was greatly influenced, I told him that the awakening came to his church not through my preaching but I believe because of the burden of one lone woman. This sister, the wife of a nobleman, had to my mind the greatest spirit of intercession and agony of any believer in the country. I found her in the different churches at all hours of the day or night where prayer meetings were being held. On one occasion, when she had been praying in a Methodist church for several hours, I spoke to her around three o'clock in the morning, quietly suggesting that she had been praying long hours and it would be good if she went home to rest. She replied through her tears, "Brother James, I cannot rest at home until God does a new thing for the spiritual life of my denomination." No wonder that later her husband's life was revolutionized during the revival and he became the mightiest evangelist of the nation!

Oh, that every reader might be willing to pay the price for revival blessing!

The Promise of Revival

Crucified

There is no gain but by a loss.
We cannot save but by the cross.
The corn of wheat, to multiply,
Must fall into the ground and die.
Oh, should a soul alone remain,
When it a hundredfold can gain?

Our souls are held by all they hold.
Slaves still are slaves in chains of gold,
To whatsoever we may cling
We make it a soul-chaining thing.
Whether it be a life or land
Or dear as our right eye or hand.

Wherever we ripe fields behold
Waving to God their sheaves of gold,
But sure some corn of wheat has died;
Some saintly soul been crucified;
Someone has suffered, wept and prayed,
And fought hell's legions undismayed.

CHAPTER 3

The Local Church, the Centre of Revival

"Revival is an assembly word. Any movement that fails to deliver the local church from its subnormal existence and raise it to a higher elevated position in its ascended Lord has no true marks of a New Testament revival.

"God's way of revival is through renewals from within, so that our local churches become the centre of blessing."

—J. A. S.

In the New Testament we discover that God's way of revival is through renewals from within, so that our local churches become the centre of blessing. A true spiritual awakening will revolutionize the spiritual life of the local evangelical churches, and then in many cases will revolutionize even liberal congregations. Any movement that fails to deliver the local church from its subnormal existence and to raise it to a higher elevated position in its ascended Lord has no true marks of a New Testament revival.

How many sincere believers are ignorant of this fundamental truth! They look for revival in the great auditorium or tent, where thousands are gathered together in a glorious evangelistic effort. The heavens are open and there is a wonderful sense of the Lord's presence in their midst, which has not been known for years. "Surely," they cry, "this is revival!" However, one of the acid tests of a true spiritual awakening is that this mighty spiritual atmosphere be taken back to the local churches.

For a mighty movement of the Spirit, it is not enough that a few isolated individual believers be revived; the evangelical local churches must be revived. Revival, as presented to us in the New Testament, is not so much an individual experience as a collective experience of a church of born-again believers. How many times down the years we have been sadly disappointed when large united meetings, which had proved such a blessing to us all, seemed to leave the local churches untouched. The casual reader of the epistles will see that the centre of all God's thought and testimony is located in these local churches. If I heard that a mighty awakening had taken place in a certain city I would not seek for revival in some great hall, rented for the purpose of evangelistic meetings: I would go direct to the evangelical churches to see the fire of God burning there.

The Promise of Revival

In the New Testament we have God's plan and purpose for His people in this dispensation of grace, even as we have in the Old Testament His plan and purpose for Israel. Pentecost marked the beginning or formation of a new body or organism which is designated by Paul as "the Church, which is His body" (Eph. 2:22, 23). Having been incorporated into Christ by the new birth (2 Cor. 5: 17), we are then incorporated into His mystical, supernatural body by the Spirit's baptism (1 Cor. 12:13). The finest description of the character and testimony of the Church is to be found in Peter's first Epistle: "But you are the elect race, the royal priesthood, the consecrated nation, the people who belong to Him, that you may proclaim the wondrous deeds of Him who has called you from darkness to His wonderful light" (1 Pet. 2:9, Moffat). This Church is composed of all believers in the Lord Jesus, both Jew and Gentile, blessed with all spiritual blessings, sealed by the Holy Spirit individually, and baptised by the Spirit collectively.

The purpose of a body is to express the character of the person who inhabits the body. The peculiar mission of the Church is to express the character and life of the Son of God, and that is why a believer taught by the Spirit will always pray, "O Lord, send revival in the body of Christ!" We affirm once again that there can be no revival anywhere other than in the Body. The purpose of the Church is to gather, through her testimony of truth and love, a people who, saved by grace, and separated by the Holy Ghost from the world, are serving the Lord and waiting for His coming (1 Thess. 1).

The Church, which is His Body, is expressed in the local churches, the members of which have been supernaturally born again and redeemed from the penalty, power and love of sin. In the New Testament we see the distinction between the Church universal and the "churches of the saints" (1 Cor. 14:33). These churches of the saints manifest the unity of the one glorious Church. The local church at Corinth, for example, was one part of the whole, and thus was a local expression and representation of the whole. Its members were in living spiritual union with every other member the whole world over. What a glorious and solemn truth! The evangelical believers in the Book of Acts were not detached isolated units, but were all vitally linked in fellowship with the "churches of the saints" in their district. "A man's body is all one, though it has a number of different organs; and all this multitude of organs goes to make up one body; so it is with Christ. We too, all of us, have been baptised into a single body by the power of a single Spirit" (1 Cor. 12:13, Knox).

In the early pages of the Book of Acts we catch the heavenly thrill of this New Testament fellowship,

> *Christ! I am Christ's! And let the name suffice you,*
> *Ay, for me too, He greatly hath sufficied;*
> *Christ is the end, for Christ was the beginning,*
> *Christ the beginning, for the end is Christ.*
>
> —MEYER

There was a holy glow in the services because the living Christ was in their midst. The Son of God was absolutely everything to them. These believers were burning with love to each other because they were burning with love to their adorable Lord.

The Promise of Revival

Then they that gladly received His word were baptised; and the same day there were added unto them about three thousand souls. And they continued steadfastly in the apostle's doctrine, and fellowship, and in breaking of bread, and in prayers. And fear came upon every soul: and many wonders and signs were done by the apostles. And all that believed were together, and had all things common; and sold their possessions and goods, and parted them to all men, as every man had need. And they, continuing daily with one accord in the temple, and breaking bread from house to house, did eat their meat with gladness and singleness of heart, praising God and having favour with all the people. And the Lord added to the church daily such as should be saved (Acts 2:41-47).

And with great power gave the apostles witness of the resurrection of the Lord Jesus: and great grace was upon them all.—4:33.

And great fear came upon all the church, and upon as many as heard these things…and of the rest durst no man join himself to them; but the people magnified them. And believers were the more added to the Lord, multitudes both of men and women. Acts 5:11-13.

Here is a thumb-nail sketch of the type of local church that revival produces.

IT WAS A STEADFAST CHURCH. These new-born babes continued. They continued steadfastly. Continuance is always the test of reality, and where a so-called revival cannot stand that test it is wise to inquire as to the cause of the failure. Sometimes a great desire to secure converts for publicity reasons robs the Gospel message of its drastic note. If we preach all the implications of the Evangel we may have fewer conversions but we will have genuine new-births. As Mr. Spurgeon said to his students, "If God enables you to build three thou sands bricks into His spiritual temple in one day, you may do it, but Peter has been the only brick-layer who has accomplished that feat up to the present. Do not go and paint the wooden wall as if it were solid stone, but let all your building be real, substantial and true, for only this kind of work is worth doing. Let all your building for God be like that of the Apostle Paul" (1 Cor. 3:9-15).

The true mark of a real work of God is the steadfast walk, day by day, of the new-born babes. *We cannot allow that backsliding is in any sense a corollary to revival.* It is only when the emotions are greatly stirred, without a deep work of grace having been wrought in the hearts of men, that backsliding is inevitable. It is an utter impossibility to avoid deep emotion in revival, as the Holy Spirit then works mightily, bringing eternal realities so vividly before the people. But the true servants of the Lord must have their animal natures crucified, so that the emotions are under the control of the Spirit of God. The work of the Spirit is quiet and deep. Any true saint who spends hours before the Throne will know that in his closet intercession it is when he is quietest in prayer that the Spirit of God is speaking most mightily to and through him. So it is in the large gatherings. Excitement must not be aimed at. There must be something more solid. Although there was great excitement and noise in these early days of the Church's history, the excitement was as incidental as is the dust when a woman sweeps the house clean. It is the steady walk that counts.

THEY CONTINUED STEADFASTLY IN THE APOSTLES' DOCTRINE AND THE APOSTLES' FELLOWSHIP. The apostles' doctrine was the doctrine they taught and preached concerning the person and work of the Lord Jesus, the Son of God. It is also called "The doctrine of Christ" in 2 John 1:9. The apostles' fellowship consisted of all those who believed the apostles' doctrine. It is not possible to be a true member of a New Testament church without believing in the apostles' doctrine. On the other hand, if one member of the assembly denies the historic fundamentals of the Christian faith that assembly ceases to be a New Testament church. *All true revival ministry is founded on the historic truths concerning our Blessed Lord:* His eternal Sonship, His virgin birth, His sinless life, His vicarious death, His bodily resurrection, and His glorious appearing. All preaching in revival times is a reaffirmation of the fundamental truths of our glorious redemption.

Vinet, in his *Outlines of Theology*, declares:

> If you learn in a general way that there has been a revival in a place, that Christianity

is reanimated, that faith has become living, and that zeal abounds—do not ask in what soil, in what system, these precious plants grow. You may be sure beforehand that it is in the rough and rugged soil of orthodoxy, under the shade of those mysteries which confound human reasoning... The revival has preached the total depravity of man and his powerlessness to save himself. The revival has preached salvation by grace and not by works, the necessity of the new birth in order to enter into the Kingdom of Heaven, and the absolute dependence of man in regard to God. The revival has preached the plenary and essential deity of Jesus Christ as well as His perfect and entire humanity; it has declared that God was in Jesus Christ, reconciling the world unto Himself and that it is in Jesus Christ alone that we have remission of sins and access to the Father; and that whosoever abideth not in Him abideth in death.

In Ephesians 2:20 we are told that the Church was "built upon the foundation of the apostles and prophets, Jesus Christ Himself being the chief cornerstone." This means that the Church was founded upon the teaching of the apostles and prophets concerning the Lord Jesus Christ. Therefore the Church was founded upon doctrine. So in a New Testament church the Word of God will be honoured and obeyed. Such will be not only a Bible-believing but a Bible-loving church. Its leaders will expound the truths of the Word of God from Genesis to Revelation. Its members will have a deep appreciation and spiritual penetration into divine Truth. Their Christian life will not be based merely upon their own experiences. They will be deep students of the Word. They will not remain babes, but will rather become giants as they digest the strong meat of the Word. How sad it is today to see around us so many believers who hardly spend a half-hour a day studying the Word for themselves. How few believers can even give a clear explanation of the truth of "adoption," and yet this is one of the most vital truths in the Christian life. Too many of our church-members remain immature, babes, requiring to be spoon-fed by their pastors for many years.

IT WAS A PRAYERFUL CHURCH. When I was a young convert the first thing that struck me when reading the Acts of the Apostles was the fact that these local assemblies lived in the atmosphere of prayer. Prayer meetings were the order of the day. They prayed on every occasion. They prayed for open doors. They prayed for guidance and boldness in their ministry after they had passed through the open doors. They prayed before the battle, during the battle, and after the battle. They prayed that God would show them His plan and that He would frustrate Satan's plan. They prayed that God would raise up workers. They prayed that God would empower workers. They prayed that God would send forth workers. They prayed in prison, and they prayed themselves out of prison. They prayed in their homes and they prayed in their church gatherings. They prayed in their private circles, and they prayed before the Sanhedrin. They lived on their knees. In order that the apostles might "give themselves continually to prayer" they appointed seven men of honest report to administer the secular business of the church. So mighty were they in prayer that they "turned the world upside down."

A true New Testament church will always be mighty in prayer. Said George Mueller, when writing to Hudson Taylor in China, "If you are going to take that province for Christ, you must go forward on your knees." One of our desperate needs is the revival of the week-night prayer meeting. How often I have heard the remark, "Only a prayer meeting." What is inferred by such a statement? Surely it implies that there is nothing important or interesting doing, as the Christians are only going to talk with God! One of the mightiest manifestations of the Spirit in revival power is the resurrection dead prayer meetings. The majority of pastors would be pleasantly shocked and surprised if even 50 percent of their congregation turned out for the week-night prayer meeting.

IT WAS AN OVERFLOWING CHURCH. They overflowed in liberality and praise. They overflowed in liberality because they overflowed in love. Their cups ran over with love to the Lord Jesus. They knew the significance of the high cost of their redemption. Gazing at Calvary, they could not hoard up their money and hold on to their lands and houses. The original text reveals that they continued to sell their property and goods and continued to bring the money and place it a t the feet of the apostles. It was not mere passing excitement, or the flush of a first love; it was a deep deep realization of the glory of their salvation that caused them to give so generously. If they had lived in our day, they would have sung heartily:

> *Everybody should know—everybody should know,*
> *I have such a wonderful Saviour, that everybody should know!*

What a great challenge to us today! *If these Christians in the first century needed to sell their possessions for the evangelization of a lost and dying world, how much more we who live in the twentieth century!* While vast continents still lie in midnight darkness, and hundreds of millions have never heard the Gospel, surely if our hearts were filled with His love and His passion we would show forth the same response. "I warn you," said A. J. Gordon, "that it will go hard with you at the judgment seat if He finds your wealth hoarded up in needless accumulations instead of being sacredly devoted to giving the Gospel to the lost."

They overflowed in *praise*. Their whole life was flooded with praise. The assembly gatherings were characterized by praise. They praised God for His glorious salvation. They praised Him that they were counted worthy to be ambassadors of the Lord Jesus. They praised Him that they could suffer shame and reproach for His glory. They praised Him that they had something to sacrifice for the spread of the Gospel. Deep spirituality and worship go hand in hand. Read the hymns of the past centuries in English, French, German, Russian, Scandinavian and Latin. Read the hymns that were born in the high days of the Church. How they overflow with deep spiritual insight and simplicity of adoration to Christ.

O God, I love Thee; not that my poor love
  May win me entrance to Thy heaven above,
Nor yet that strangers to Thy love must know
  The bitterness of everlasting woe.

But Jesus, Thou art mine, and I am Thine;
  Clasped to Thy bosom by Thy arms divine,
Who on the cruel cross for me hast borne
  The nails, the spear, and man's unpitying scorn.

No thought can fathom, and no tongue express
  Thy grief, Thy toils, Thy anguish measureless;
Thy death, O Lamb of God, the undefiled —
  And all for me, Thy wayward sinful child!

How can I choose but love Thee, God's dear Son,
  O Jesus, loveliest and most loving one!
Were there no heaven to gain, no hell to flee,
  For what Thou art alone, I must love Thee.

Not for the hope of glory or reward,
  But even as Thy self hast loved me, Lord
I love Thee, and will love Thee and adore
  Who art my King, my God, for evermore.

How little praise there is in our churches today! How refreshing it would be for a group of churches to come together for a united praise meeting. Such words related to the word "praise" as price, prize, precious, appraise, appreciate, etc., help us to understand better the full meaning of the term. The saints bursting forth spontaneously into songs of adoration and worship is one of the glories of revival. Song leaders are not necessary during such times, as the huge congregations sing over and over again the songs of Zion which spring from their hearts. I remember once dismissing an immense congregation in Czechoslovakia twice in a single evening without any success. I had finished preaching and pronounced the benediction twice, but the believers went on praising the Lord for over an hour after I had left the building. In times of revival the Holy Spirit inspires a great number of hymns to be written. For every John Wesley there is a Charles Wesley:

> *Oh, for a thousand, tongues to sing*
> *My great Redeemer's praise!*
> *The glories of my God and King,*
> *The triumphs of His grace.*

IT WAS A POWERFUL CHURCH.

It was powerful in its Gospel presentation. In one day three thousand souls were saved, and on another day about five thousand men and women. Today if a church of three thousand members won one hundred and twenty souls to Christ in one day some would call that revival! Oh, dear child of God, a church that is not a soul-winning church is not a New Testament church. It is true that there are times of sowing as well as times of reaping, but every pastor and every group of believers should search their hearts industriously to see why there is a dearth of conversions. It seems that Satan has so drugged the Lord's dear ones that they have no deep concern and anguish in their lack of spiritual results. How many assemblies accept with astonishing calmness annual reports of so few, if any, conversions! Such churches should convene special meetings in desperation before the Lord to see if there is anything hindering God's blessing His Word according to Acts 4:33, "And with great power gave the apostles witness of the resurrection of the Lord Jesus, and great grace was upon them all."

How inconsistent it is for churches back home, who very rarely ever see the Lord add to their membership, to expect a mighty harvest to be reaped by the missionaries they support laboring in hostile heathen lands! If they demand and expect a mighty manifestation of the power of the Gospel among the pagan population, should they not expect a mightier demonstration in an evangelical atmosphere?

They were powerful in their holiness. "Great awe came over the whole church, and over all that heard about this…though the people extolled them, not a soul from the outside dared to join them. On the other hand, crowds of men and women who believed in the Lord were brought in" (Moffat). It was a powerful Church because of the presence of the Holy Spirit in their midst. The sin of Ananias and Sapphira was a frontal attack by Satan to deny the deity of the Holy Spirit. When judgment was brought to bear upon these two, a holy awe fell upon saved and unsaved alike. So holy was this church that hypocrites and unbelievers dared not join themselves to it. On the other hand, crowds of men and women who were true believers were brought in.

How easy it is to receive the "right hand of fellowship" in our churches today! Without doubt this weakness is one of the underlying causes of the subnormal church. Too many people are rushed to the altar. Too many people are rushed into church-membership without careful examination and instruction. In our evangelical churches of Eastern Europe and Russia, sometimes it takes from six months to a year for a new convert to be received into church-membership. So holy and powerful are these churches in their Gospel witness that the unsaved attending their services know that it is no small thing to enlist under the banner of the Lord and identify themselves with a company of born-again believers.

One of the mightiest warnings of A. J. Gordon to the church is as follows:

> We dwell much upon the attractions of Christianity, but rarely stop to think that it may also have repulsions, which are vitally necessary to its purity and permanence. If the Church of Christ draws to herself that which she cannot assimilate to herself, her life is at once imperilled; for the body of believers must be at one with itself, though it be at war with the world. Its purity and its power depend, firs t of all, upon its unity. So that if perchance the Church shall attract without at the same time transforming them; if she shall attach them to her membership without assimilating them to her life—she has only weakened herself by her increase, and diminished herself by her additions. Such is the

lesson that is impressed upon us by the text "and of the rest durst no man join himself to them."

The Church has just entered upon her first conquest. The Gospel is preached with a freeness and breadth of offer unheard of before. Three thousand souls have been added to the Church in a single day. The tide of success is rising higher. The sect of the Nazarenes is fairly becoming popular. Multitudes are crowding up to lay their gifts at the apostle's feet. Is there not a danger that the infant Church may be overwhelmed in the tide of her own prosperity? That upon the swelling wave of success the uncircumcised and the unclean may be born into her communion to corrupt and destroy it? But look! Like a keen lightning flash the judgment of God falls in the midst of His mercies, and the two who had "agreed together to tempt the Spirit of the Lord" lie dead at the apostles' feet. Is God about to close the gate of mercy so recently opened, and to guard it with a flaming sword? No! Here is an exhibition of His holiness in the midst of His free grace. And before this unsheathed sword of His holiness the multitude instantly divides—apart thrust back, apart drawn nearer. No sincere disciples are repelled, for the record is that "believers were the more added to the Lord, multitudes of both men and women."

The terror of the Lord puts afar off those who have not the love of the Lord to bring them nigh. My brethren, I know of no lesson concerning the growth and development of Christ's Church that needs to be more thoughtfully pondered than this. The tendency of our times is to multiply the attractions of Christianity. No attraction can be too powerful, no charm can be too alluring that acts for the single ends of drawing believers to Christ and identifying them with His Body. *But the appeals which win men without transforming them, which join them to the Church without bringing them into fellow ship with Christ, are fatal to a pure Christianity, and in the end must put the very existence of the Church in jeopardy.* In the first place, the sanctity of life and character which Christ requires in His Church is her most powerful defence. These, O Church of God, are thy weapons of defence and conquest! I believe that the most effective discipline which any church can have is a consecrated and devoted and unworldly piety in its members.

Whenever we see God's wonderful pattern for the Church so practically demonstrated in these pages in the Book of Acts we cry with Jeremiah, "How is the gold become dim! How is the most fine gold changed!"

CHAPTER 4

Worldliness and Revival

"I looked for the Church and I found it in the world;
I looked for the world, and alas, I found it in the Church."

— ANDREW BONAR

"Worldliness is an atmosphere in which one lives and which robs the Christian life of its radiant, dynamic character."

— J. A. S.

From the broken heart of Jehovah comes the scathing rebuke to His people: "For my people have committed two evils; they have forsaken Me, the fountain of living waters, and hewed them out cisterns, broken cisterns, that can hold no water" (Jer. 2:13).

Today how many believers have forsaken the Lord Jesus, the Fountain of all true satisfaction and heart-rest, and are seeking joy in worldly pleasures! They profess to love Him and serve Him, and yet they have allowed the attractions of this world to dim their spiritual eyesight. Worldliness robs the Christian life of its vital radiant dynamic character. Worldliness is anything that takes the keen edge off my spiritual life and dims my vision of the Lord. Worldliness is anything that robs me of my deep inner love-life with my glorious Redeemer. Worldliness is anything that takes away my burden for souls. Worldliness is anything that hinders my spending time in the closet in earnest intercession, by the power of the Spirit, for the Church and the world.

> *Whatever passes as a cloud between*
> *The mental eye of faith and things unseen,*
> *Causing that brighter world to disappear,*
> *Or seem less lovely, or its hope less dear;*
> *THAT is our world—our idol, though it bear*
> *Affection's impress or devotion's air.*

The curse of worldliness has invaded the Church. We must enter a crusade against it. We cannot be neutral. We cannot be silent. It is a matter of life and death. The Church is slowly being choked to death in the atmosphere of worldliness. Worldliness robs the Church of its purity and power, and places her in a position where she cannot be a true bride of the Lord. It places her in a position where she cannot proclaim the whole counsel of God. In the study of Church history we find that the pilgrim Church never had so much power over the world as when she had nothing to do with it!

The end times are upon us, and Satan is employing every means possible to crowd the Lord out of the lives of His saints.

He is finding very effective means, for instance, his scheme of invading their homes through the medium of the television.

The vast majority of evangelicals who would not for one moment visit places of worldly amusement allow the same places to enter their homes through the medium of television. The popular programmes have more power over many of God's children than the week-night prayer meetings. Many "Television Christians" know better the names of current film stars, comedians, sportsmen and politicians than they know the names and characters of the Bible.

There is an established pattern that has settled in our evangelical churches all over the North American Continent. The majority of members attend the service on Sunday morning. Less than fifty per cent attend the evening Gospel service. Less than twenty per cent attend the only week-night praying meeting of the assembly. Thousands of hours each year are forever lost over worldly television programmes, which should have been spent in deep spiritual conversation, study of the Word, and glorious communion with the Lord. Surely the hardest and most discouraging task on earth today is to be assigned by the Head of the Church to shepherd such flocks. I had far rather face a Soviet firing squad than to be the pastor of such a people. I had rather spend five years in a Soviet prison camp than five years as pastor of some of these churches!

We know of one pastor who could not understand why his prayers for revival in his church were not being answered, even though he and his wife fasted and prayed far into the night. One Sunday, on his way to the prayer meeting before the evening service, he visited some of his best members, who had not been present in the service that morning. He feared they were ill. Imagine his dismay and astonishment when he discovered that they and four other church families had settled down for the evening around a worldly television show.

We know of another pastor who went a great distance to visit some of his members in order to read and pray with them, as is the custom with every holy man of God. They welcomed him and served him coffee, but gave him no time to talk with them about the Lord. They had their favourite television programme on and did not offer to turn it off during the whole visit. There was no opportunity for spiritual conversation, and the pastor left with a terrible sense of frustration. The tragedy was that these dear evangelicals felt no sense of shame that they had allowed a programme to crowd out the Lord that day, as such action was their normal daily routine.

If Andrew Bonar could say seventy years ago: "I looked for the Church and I found it in the world; I looked for the world, and alas, I found it in the Church!" what would this dear man of God say to us today? When I see these starry-eyed evangelical television fans wasting precious hours that could be spent more profitably the words of Paul to the Galatians keep coming to my mind, "O SENSELESS Galatians, who hath bewitched you—you who have Jesus Christ the crucified placarded before your eyes?" (Gal. 3:1, Moffat). Who has been casting a spell over you? Surely today it is Satan, through the eyegate!

We can easily understand how revival came among the Methodists in Britain when they sang lustily with Charles Wesley:

Vain delusive world, adieu,
With all of creature good.
Only Jesus I pursue
Who bought me with His blood.
All thy pleasures I forgo,
I trample on thy wealth and pride,
Only Jesus would I know,
And Jesus crucified.

This worldliness dims the vision of the saints and causes them to lose the sense of eternal values. They become eccentric in the sight of God and the holy angels. They forget that they have been purchased to be possessed. They have lost their pilgrim status. There is no longer a distinction between them and the worldlings. They no longer live as aliens and exiles. Although they profess to the unsaved that they are "strangers and pilgrims," people in a strange land, and on their way home to "The Celestial City, alas, the world does not believe them. Like Lot of old, they have lost their testimony.

Again, because the spirit of worldliness has invaded the Church, there is so little sacrifice in the average Christian life. The church is too comfortable and cosy. "Moab hath been at ease from his youth, and he has settled on his lees" (Jer. 48:11). Each pastor knows he has two congregations; the congregation of "the dead" and the congregation of "the living." Like Gideon, we need to have a revival by subtraction. No wonder the early Methodists had revival. John Wesley gives us the secret in a diary entry: "Visited a Society today. It had thirty-two members: stroked off twenty. Glory to God!"

James Alexander Stewart

If Christians were half as much excited about their heavenly heritage as they are about their earthly possessions they would be branded at once as fanatics. Amy Carmichael wrote:

> We who follow the Crucified are n o t here to make a pleasant thing of life; we are called to suffer for the sake of a suffering sinful world. The Lord forgive us our shameful evasions and hesitations. His brow was crowned with thorns; do we seek rosebuds for our crowning? His hands were pierced with nails; are our hands ringed with jewels? His feet were bare and bound; do our feet walk delicately? What do we know of travail? Of tears that scald before they fall? Of heartbreak? Of being scorned? God forgive us our love of ease! God forgive us that so often we turn our face from life that is even remotely like His. Forgive us that we all but worship comfort, the delight of the presence of loved ones, possessions, treasures on earth. Far, far from our prayers, too often is any thought of prayer for a love which will lead us to give one whom we love; to follow our Lord to Gethsemane, to Calvary—perhaps because we have never been there ourselves.
>
> *From subtle, love of softening things,*
> *From easy choices, weakenings*
> *(Not thus are spirits fortified,*

The Promise of Revival

*Not this way went the Crucified),
From all that dims Thy Calvary,
O Lamb of God, deliver me!*

The love of the things of this world robs the Church of her passion for souls. Few church members take more than casual interest in the salvation of souls. Many of us have ceased to be amazed at the in difference without because there is so much apathy with in. When I see a vacant seat in the prayer meeting I say to myself, "There is a vote against revival." When I see an empty place in the Gospel service on the Lord's Day evening I say to myself, "There is a vote against revival." When I see a Sunday School class left without a teacher I say to myself, "There is a vote against revival." When I hear of church members who leave the place of prayer for places of amusement I count up so many votes against the Lord's coming in revival power among us.

My friend, Hyman Appelman, tells the following story:

> One of my truly great preacher friends relates an incident in one of his campaigns somewhere in Oklahoma. He had tried earnestly to get the church-people to visit, to invite the lost to the services, but very few responded. There came the week's half-holiday. A barber in that town, with several of his friends, went on a fishing trip. The boat overturned, drowning the barber. Everything in that town stopped as the lake was searched for the body. They hired a diver at $100.00 per day. On the fourth day

the body was located. As the people slowly walked past the open coffin in the church, the pastor was heard to say softly, "Oh, Sam, if these people had cared as much for your soul as they do for your dead body you wouldn't be in hell now!" How true! How tragically, bitterly true!

The Church of God must robe herself in sackcloth. The Church of God must make a public confession of her awful position of back-sliding. For a Christian redeemed by Calvary's blood to live a worldly life is treason and spiritual suicide. It is better to be poor with Philadelphia than to become rich with Laodicea. It is better to be branded a fanatic than to be at ease in Zion.

"Go a little deeper," said a French soldier at Austerlitz, to the surgeon who was probing his left side for a bullet. "Go a little deeper, and you will find the Emperor." Oh that this were true with every child of God! Oh that we all could say with Paul: "For me to live means Christ." The love of Christ overwhelms and overmasters me! I have only one purpose in life and that is to live for the One who died, rose again, ascended, and is coming back for me! The greatest calling of every Christian is to live abundantly, actively, aggressively, joyfully, NOW, in the power of the Holy Spirit.

The Promise of Revival

Let me love Thee, Thou are claiming
  Every feeling on my soul;
Let me love, in power prevailing,
  Render Thee my life, my all;
For life's burdens they are easy,
  And life's sorrows lose their sting
If they're carried, Lord, to please Thee,
  If they're done Thy smile to win.

Let me love Thee—come revealing
  All Thy love has done for me;
Help my doubt, so unbelieving
  By the sight of Calvary;
Let me see Thy love despising
  All the shame my sins have brought,
By Thy torment realizing
  What a price my burden bought.

Let me love Thee, love is mighty, —
  Swaying realms of deed and thought,
By which I shall walk uprightly
  And shall serve Thee as I ought.
Love will soften every sorrow,
  Love will lighten every care,
Love unquestioning will follow,
  Love will triumph, love will bear.

James Alexander Stewart

Chorus
Let me love Thee, Saviour
　Take my heart forever,
Nothing but Thy favour, Lord,
　My soul can satisfy!
　　　—W. M. BOOTH-CLIBBORN

CHAPTER 5

The Holy Spirit and Revival

"There are even now seasons of extraordinary communion with the Lord, when, through the Holy Spirit, He is pleased to manifest Himself to the soul in such unwonted power that they may be truly called 'times of refreshing.'"

—A. J. GORDON

"There can be no revival a part from the Holy Ghost; He is the author of every Heaven-sent movement."

—J. A. S.

There can be no revival apart from the Holy Spirit. He is the author of every Heaven-sent movement. There can be no quickening to abundant life among the saints, or spiritual resurrection of the unsaved, apart from the supernatural work of the Executive Member of the Godhead. So, in seeking the Father's face for revival, we must honour and obey this blessed Comforter, who is the Administrator of the affairs of the Church.

In the pages of the New Testament we see that every grace of the Christian life is attributed to the indwelling power of an ungrieved Spirit. The Holy Spirit is the One who glorifies the Lord Jesus in the experience of every child of God. The Saviour predicted, "When the Comforter is come, whom I will send unto you of the Father, He shall testify of me" (John 15:26). It is the whole work of the Comforter to bear witness of Christ, to reveal Christ, and to glorify Christ in our experience. We will never really know Him except by direct revelation of the Spirit. We may listen, at Conventions, to others speaking about Him, but unless the Heavenly Teacher Himself interprets and applies the message of God to our own souls we can never really know Christ.

Not only does the Spirit reveal Christ, but He also forms the indwelling Christ in our hearts and minds. Our Redeemer promised in His Paschal discourse, "I will not leave you comfortless. I will come to you." He would come to them by the Person of the Holy Spirit, who is now the vice-regent of Christ. When the Comforter comes He forms within the believer the living Christ. Paul prays for the saints at Ephesus, "to be strengthened by His Spirit with power penetrating to your inmost being" (Eph. 3:16, Weymouth). To what purpose? "That Christ may make His home in your hearts through your faith" (v. 17). This is the true secret of all practical scriptural holiness. We can never attain to true holiness by our own efforts and striving, but only by surrendering to the Holy Spirit to form the indwelling Christ within.

The Holy Spirit is not only the Agent for our sanctification, but He is also the Divine Helper in the ministry of intercession. "The Spirit comes to the aid of our weakness; when we do not know what prayer to offer, to pray as we ought, the Spirit Himself intercedes for us, with groans beyond all utterance: and God, who can read our hearts, knows well what the Spirit's intent is; for indeed it is according to the mind of God that He makes intercession for the saints" (Rom. 8:26-27, Knox). Nowhere in the Christian life are we so baffled and beaten as when we seek to intercede on behalf of a languishing Church and a lost and dying world. How comforting it is to know that the heavenly Paraclete is the One who comes alongside to help us in this ministry, by prompting and energizing our prayers.

Not only in our Christian walk do we need the Holy Spirit, but also in our Christian service. All true longings for the salvation of the lost are nothing less than the passion of Christ, reproduced in us by the power of the Spirit. It is only a Spirit-filled believer that can truly say: "I say the truth in Christ, I lie not, my conscience also bearing me witness in the Holy Ghost, that I have great heaviness and continual sorrow in my heart, for I could wish that myself were accursed from Christ for my brethren, my kinsmen according to the flesh" (Rom. 9:1-3). If we try to work up a passion for souls it will be only mere fleshly emotion. Only our mighty Intercessor can give us this burden.

Apart from the mighty enduement of power from the Spirit of Pentecost, all our Gospel service will be in vain. The natural, unregenerated man cannot comprehend "the things of the Spirit." His darkened mind can only be enlightened by the divine intervention of God, the Holy Ghost. He cannot be argued, fascinated, "bullied" or "enthused" into accepting Christ as his Saviour. It is not enough that we clearly expound the Gospel. It must be given in the demonstration and power of the Spirit and applied by Him. Paul wrote to the Thessalonians, "Our Gospel came not unto you in word only, but also in power, and in the Holy Ghost" (1 Thess. 1:5). Peter reminded the sojourners of the dispersion that the Gospel had been preached to them "with the Holy Ghost sent down from heaven" (1 Pet. 1:12). The sin that damns the soul is the rejection of Christ as Lord and Saviour. This sin of disbelieving on Christ is THE great sin, because it summarizes all other sins. Only the Holy Spirit can convict a lost soul of the sin of Christ-rejection and lead him to the foot of the Cross. As no person can be saved a part from the redemptive work of Christ, so also can no one be saved a part from the regenerating work of the Spirit. "And He when He is come, will convict the world in respect of sin, and of righteousness, and of judgment" (John 16:8, R.V.). When asked on various occasions to speak at the preparatory meetings before the commencement of large evangelistic campaigns, I have seen the astonishment come over the faces of the Christian workers when I declared that there can be no revival among the saints and no regeneration among the unsaved apart from the work of the Holy Spirit. Many sincere, enthusiastic Christian workers have been deeply perturbed and even offended, and some have even gone so far as to accuse me of preaching a very discouraging doctrine when I insisted on this fact. Surely this is the first and foremost fact that every Christian worker must face in his service for God. I remember in one town being asked not to speak again to these preparatory groups, as I was only discouraging them in the work of the Lord. It is true that the Lord uses human instruments for the salvation of souls, but it is only when these instruments are yielded to His control that they can point guilty sinners to the Lamb of God.

> *No awful sense we find of sin,*
>   *The sinful life and sinful heart;*
> *No loathing of the plague within,*
>   *Until the Lord that feel impart;*
> *But when the Spirit of Truth is come*
>   *A sinner trembles at his doom.*
>
> *Convinced and pierced through and through,*
>   *He thinks himself the sinner chief;*
> *And, conscious of his mighty woe,*
>   *Perceives at length his unbelief;*
> *Good creeds may stock his head around,*
>   *But in his heart no faith is found.*
>
> *No power his nature can afford*
>   *To change his heart, or purge his guilt;*
> *No help is found but in the Lord,*
>   *No balm but in the blood He spilt;*
> *A ruined soul, condemned he stands,*
>   *And unto Jesus lifts his hands.*
>
> —BERRIDGE

Since there can be no awakening among believers and no regeneration of the lost apart from the supernatural workings of the Holy Ghost in and through the saints, it behooves every child of God to seek earnestly the enduement of power for his walk and witness. We do not imply that it is God's will that all have the same empowering experience which George Whitefield or James Brainerd Taylor received, or that all shall be carried up to the highest heavens as were Samuel Rutherford and Adelaide Newton, but we do insist that the anointing of the Spirit is needed to fit each one of us for the highest service in the work to which God has called us. I believe, from my study of the Word, and from a careful examination of the innerexperiences of holy men and women of God, that this mighty baptism is just as real an experience as that of regeneration itself.

A careful reader of the Scriptures need not be told how closely the ceremony of anointing was related to all the important offices and ministries of the servant of Jehovah under the old Covenant.

> The priest was anointed that he might be holy unto the Lord (Lev. 8:12).
>
> The king was anointed that the Spirit of the Lord might rest upon him in power (1 Sam. 16:15).
>
> The prophet was anointed that he might be the oracle of God to the people (1 Sam. 19:16).

No servant of Jehovah was deemed qualified for his ministry without this holy sanctified touch laid upon him. Imagine, if you can, a priest attempting to minister before the Lord and daring to touch the holy things of the sanctuary without having first of all been sprinkled with the holy anointing oil! God was so jealous for the sanctity of those who had been anointed for service that the penalty of failing to wash the hands and feet when they ministered before the Lord was death (Exod. 30:19-21). What, then, but death in its most awful form must have been the penalty of such presumption as that which we have suggested? The holy anointing was the outward, visible sign of the impartation to the priests of those gifts and graces which qualified them for being the ministers of the Lord, the teachers, the guides, and the intercessors of the Lord's people.

Under the new economy every born-again, blood-washed child of God is a royal priest to minister before and for the Lord, and hence needs the anointing of the Spirit. The Church is a kingdom of priests, and each individual believer is a royal priest (Rev. 1:6; 1 Pet. 2:9).

It is necessary for us to inquire concerning what preparation our Lord received to fully equip Him for His ministry here on earth. I believe that He is our example in all things. "It is," says Pascal, "one of the great principles of Christianity that whatever happened to Jesus Christ on earth should come to pass in the souls and bodies of all that are His." One of the profound mysteries in the New Testament is that Christ needed to be anointed by the Spirit. Apart from the incarnation, no truth drives me to my knees in such adoration and worship as this amazing fact. The sinless, sovereign One, the One who always pleased the Father, the One to whom the Spirit was given without measure, must at His inauguration for His mediatorial work as Prophet, Priest and King receive a mighty enduement of power! As I arise from my knees with the awe of God upon my soul, I breathe reverently the following words:

"How amazing that my blessed Lord, my Kinsman Redeemer, needed this Baptism."

If any Christian worker doubts that this is the true interpretation of the heavenly dove alighting upon the Son of God he needs only turn to the words of Peter for a full explanation: "How God anointed Jesus of Nazareth with the Holy Ghost and with power; who went about doing good and healing all that were oppressed with the devil" (Acts 10:38). Oh, dear child of God, if our Kinsman Redeemer could not begin His public ministry without this anointing, how can we be so presumptuous as to think that we can accomplish any work that can stand the scrutiny at Christ's judgment seat if we ignore this baptism! Too many are content to claim their share in Calvary who never go further and claim their share in the gift of Pentecost. They are content with the brazen altar, but never seek to enter into the "holiest of all." The Upper Room discourse of our Lord proves that it was His clear intention, through His ascension, to claim for His whole Church the same anointing of the Spirit as He Himself had received at His baptism."The Spirit of the Lord is upon me, because He has anointed me to preach" (Luke 4:18). The oil that anointed the head of our great High Priest was intended to fall upon us also, who are but as the hem of His garment.

Is there not a danger in these momentous days of the atomic and space age that we spend our time disputing about the power of the Spirit ?In his day Dr. A. T. Pierson said that while theologians were contending as to what the Baptism of the Spirit was, and were divided on the question as to whether it was proper to expect or even to ask for it in this dispensation, the incontrovertible fact was that men and women were both asking for and receiving a new and strange investment of power from on high, which somehow revolutionized their character, conduct, temper, and work. Said he, "We may best stop our discussion and go to praying." So deeply exercised was this precious man of God, that at the very height of his popularity he sat down and wrote his resignation from every committee on which he had been placed in order that he might give more time, himself, to this urgent need.

Too often even missionaries in the foreign mission field lapse into what we call a mere perfunctory routine of work which, among all Christian workers, is the most subtle of all snares.

Pilkington of Uganda declared that "But for the Spirit's special enduement that came upon me during a crisis in my life as a missionary, I would have been compelled to abandon the field and return home as a failure."

The evangelical Church today is far removed from her Pentecostal prototype. Hudson Taylor, at a Conference in New York in 1901, uttered these stirring words of challenge, out of a wealth of experience: "Today, the Holy Ghost is as truly available an d as mighty in power as He was on the Day of Pentecost. But has the whole Church ever, since the days before Pentecost, put aside every other work and waited for Him for ten days, that the power might be manifested? Has there not been a source of failure here? We have given too much attention to methods and machinery and to human resources, and too little to the source of power, the Blessed Spirit." The message of the Acts of the Apostles is that the bare simplicities of the Gospel are the Things that count. The Glory of that dynamic Church was that transformed men proclaimed the Gospel with holy unction and certified it with holy lives. Our desperate need today is for a fresh enduement of power. This will be the authentic touch of God upon our lives.

The story is told of a noble woman in London city who after years of great usefulness in the service of the Lord was translated to glory. They carried her body into one of the greatest auditoriums that the city and the world might p ay her honour. Lords and ladies and royalty came to pay tribute. The rich people of Britain and Europe came to look and weep. Then the poor people came pressing their way into the great building. The weeping thousands passed beside the sleeping woman. At last, a poor woman made her way down the aisle. She had every mark of poverty as she carried a child in one arm and led another by the hand. When she reached the coffin, she put the baby on the floor, loosed the clasp of the older child's hand and then stooped to kiss the glass which covered the face, while the multitude sobbed in sympathy with her.

Who was she, sleeping in the coffin yonder? Why, none other than Mrs. Catherine Booth, the mother of the Salvation Army, one of the grandest women that God ever called into His service. The effectiveness of Catherine Booth's ministry is a true example of what the Holy Spirit can do in and through a human life, surrendered and obedient to His control.

Andrew Murray helpfully suggests the way into a fresh enduement of power by the following directions:

1. *I believe that there Holy Spirit and enduement with power.*
2. *I believe it is for me!*
3. *I have never received it; or if I have received it once, I have lost it.*
4. *I long and desire to secure it at all costs; and am prepared to surrender whatever hinders.*
5. *I do now humbly and thankfully open my heart to receive all that I believe my Saviour is waiting to give; and even if there be no result in the emotion I will still believe that I have received, according to Mark 11:24.*

Let us now go on our knees and pray reverently in the words of William Pennefather, the Church of England clergyman, whose ministry through the Mildmay Conference Movement lifted the evangelical Church of Great Britain to glorious heights some seventy years ago:

> *Oh, Lord, with one accord*
>   *We gather round Thy Throne*
> *To hear Thy Holy Word,*
>   *To worship Thee alone.*
> *Now send from heaven the Holy Ghost,*
>   *Be this another Pentecost!*
>
> *We have no strength to meet*
>   *The storms that round us lower;*

James Alexander Stewart

Keep Thou our trembling feet
    In every trying hour;
More than victorious shall we be
If girded with Thy panoply.

Where is the mighty wind
    That shook the Holy Place,
That gladdened every mind
    And brightened every face?
Where are the cloven tongues of flame
That marked each follower of the Lamb?

There is no change in Thee,
    Lord God, the Holy Ghost!
    Thy glorious majesty
    Is as at Pentecost.
Oh, may our loosened tongues proclaim
That Thou, our God, art still the same!

And may that living wave,
    Which issues from on high,
Whose golden waters lave
    Thy Throne eternally,
Flow down in power on us today,
That none may go unblest away!

The Promise of Revival

Anoint us with Thy grace,
    To yield ourselves to Thee;
To run our daily race,
    With joy and energy,
Until we hear the Bridegroom say,
"Rise up, my love, and come away."

CHAPTER 6

Satan's Great Snare in Times of Revival

"The Spirit may be grieved by a spirit of boasting about the revival. Sometimes, as soon as revival commences, you will see it blazed out in the newspapers. Most commonly, this publicity will kill the revival."

—CHARLES FINNEY

"It is a sign of immaturity and carnality for Christians to idolize the instruments of God."

—J. A. S.

The message of this book would not be complete without our having left the reader with a warning concerning the reality of Satan's personality, activity and subtlety. He is the arch-enemy of the Church, and the great antagonist of the Son of God. The Word of God abounds with warnings concerning his aggressive attacks against the Church of Jesus Christ. We find in these warnings that Satan's business is to deceive the saints by different stratagems. For example, Paul writes to the Corinthian believers that they should forgive one another, "lest Satan should get an advantage of us, for we are not ignorant of his devices" (2 Cor. 2:11). He exhorts the Ephesian believers to "put on the whole armour of God, that ye may be able to stand against the wiles of the devil" (Eph. 6:11). The word "wiles" suggests a method or a cunning device of Satan which he uses to beguile the saints (see 2 Cor. 11:3).

One device of the devil is to get the believers proud of "their revival" and proud of their revival leaders. He suggests that it would be good and glorifying to God to publicize in a large way the wonders of the workings of His grace. Oftentimes, however, lurking at the back of this is self-exaltation, self-glory, and self-aggrandizement. It is well always to remember that the less we court publicity, when the Holy Spirit is doing His strange work, the purer and more lasting will be the results.

As we have mentioned in the previous chapter, the mighty workings of God's Holy Spirit is alone the efficient cause of revival. This truth, rightly understood, would rescue us from the folly and danger of attaching too much value to the use of the human instruments. We are too prone to overestimate, and even sometimes to idolize, these chosen vessels until God has to cast them aside that He may rescue us from such a dangerous delusion. We must never forget that no creature possesses or can possess any inherent value, and that all virtue, all power, and all glory belongs to God alone forever.

The Promise of Revival

Christ always comes in lowly guise, and always brings His cross with Him. No one who has been used by God in revival ministry can ever forget the melting, the brokenness, and the humiliation before Him. Spontaneous, New Testament revivals begin in the secret of holy obscurity, with insignificant and broken instruments; instruments which have passed through a Gethsemane experience and have become worms before a Great God. Great respect is certainly due to these blessed men and women of God, but we must be careful never to magnify them in an idolatrous way, as the world worships its film stars and sportsmen, and its heroes. When such idolatry takes place, the Holy Spirit is grieved and quenched and soon withdraws Himself from the revival movement.

"Let us make here three tabernacles, one for Thee, one for Moses and one for Elias!" cried Peter on the mount. While he was yet speaking these idolatrous words, a bright cloud obliterated the Christian leaders, and a voice from the most excellent glory announced sternly, "This is My Beloved Son."

When Bartimaeus asked what the commotion about him meant, the preachers did not answer, "We are passing by." True, it was their movements that arrested the blind man. He heard them. But when he asked what caused the commotion of the multitude, he was told, "Jesus of Nazareth passeth by." Here is the secret of all true reports about revival:

" JESUS OF NAZARETH PASSETH BY " (Luke 18:37).

> *What meaneth this eager, anxious throng?*
> *What moves with busy haste along?*
> *These wondrous gatherings day by day?*

James Alexander Stewart

What means the strong commotion, pray?
In accents hushed, the throng reply:
—"JESUS OF NAZARETH PASSETH BY."

It is said that the famous Russian masters, when painting the figures of Christ on their Greek Catholic Icons, would never sign their names to their work. When asked why, they replied, "How could we place our names beside the figure of the glorious Redeemer!"

How we all, leaders and people alike, need to pray constantly with the late Ruth Paxson, "O Lord, never let me ever touch Thy glory!"

Oh, beloved, it is only when revival is a matter of history that it may become the subject of applause. Charles Finney has said:

> If anything is to be said about revival, give only the plain and naked facts, just as they are, and let them pass for what they are worth.
>
> When Christians get proud of their "great revival," it will cease. I mean those Christians who have been instrumental in promoting it. It is almost always the case in revival that a part of the Church proves too proud or too worldly to take any part in the work. They are determined to stand aloof and wait to see what it will come to. The pride of this part of the Church cannot stop the revival, for the

revival never rested on them. They may fold their arms and do nothing but look out and find fault; and still the work may go on.

But when the part of the Church that does the work begins to think what a great revival they have had, how they have laboured and prayed, how bold and zealous they have been, and how much good they have done, then the work will be likely to decline. Perhaps it has been published in the papers as to what a great revival there has been in a certain church and how absorbed the members have been, so they think how high they will stand in the estimation of other churches and the revival ceases.

The Spirit may be grieved by a spirit of boasting about the revival. Sometimes, as soon as a revival commences, you will see it blazed out in the newspapers. And most commonly this will kill the revival. There was a case in a neighbouring state where revival commenced, and instantly there came out a letter from the pastor telling that he had a revival. I saw the letter, and I said to myself, " That is the last that we shall hear of his revival." And so it was. In a few days the work totally ceased. I could mention cases and places where persons enjoy the presence of God. The Spirit withdraws from them all over the land, because they have had such a great revival. And so they get puffed up and vain, and they can no longer have published such things as to puff up the church, and to make the people so proud that little more could be done for the revival.

Some, under pretence of publishing things to the praise and glory of God, have published things that savoured so strongly of a disposition to exalt themselves—making their own agency stand out conspicuously—as were evidently calculated to make an unhappy impression. At a protracted meeting held in this church a year ago last fall there were five hundred hopefully converted, whose names and places of residence we knew. A considerable number of them joined this church. Many of them united with other churches. Nothing was said of this in the papers. I have several times been asked why we were so silent on this subject. *I could only reply that there was such a tendency to self-exaltation in the churches that I was afraid to publish anything on the subject.*

May God deliver us from immodest and sensational publicity! May we remember the solemn words of warning as found in the Old Testament scriptures: "And now, O ye priests, this commandment is for you. If ye will not hear, and if ye will not lay it to heart, to give glory unto My name, saith the Lord of Hosts, I will even send a curse upon you, and

I will curse your blessings; yea, I have cursed them already because ye do not lay it to heart" (Mai. 2:1, 2).

" I am the Lord, that is My name, and My glory will I not give to an other" (Isa. 42:8).

CHAPTER 7

An Urgent Appeal

"The day of Pentecost was a pattern day; all the days of this dispensation should have been like it, or should have exceeded it. But alas, the church has fallen down to the state in which it was before this blessing was bestowed, and it is necessary for us to ask Christ to begin over again."
—GEORGE BOWEN

"God loves unity, and so He loves a united cry; a petition signed by more than one."
—ANDREW BONAR

In 1724 Jonathan Edwards, in the midst of the mightiest awakening ever known on the North American Continent, after much fasting and prayer, sent out his famous appeal for Christians of all lands to unite together to pray for a world-wide awakening and a return to primitive apostolic Christianity. A copy of this manifesto fell into the hands of William Carey, a modest English shoemaker, who was stirred to his deepest depths. He gathered a little group of believers together in his home to pray that God would do "a new thing" in their midst. Later, Carey republished Edwards' revival appeal, to which may be traced the mighty movements of the Spirit which so characterized the nineteenth century, and also the world-wide missionary crusade, which was the most conspicuous feature of that period. William Carey became the father of modern missions.

Later still this same manifesto was used by God to change the spiritual life of Charles Finney, a converted young lawyer of New York State. Finney based all his revival-reasonings on this document. Jonathan Edwards' burden for revival caught fire in the heart of this young prophet, and once again revival fires began to burn in North America.

And later again, when President Finney was on a Mediterranean holiday for the recuperation of his health, the Holy Ghost so burdened him about the spiritual "slump" of the sub-normal churches of North America that he began to prepare his now famous Lectures on Revival. These revival lectures have been read by Christian workers all over the world, and through their heart-warming messages revivals have broken out in many local churches and mission stations. This text book has appeared in every leading language. Sometimes there has been printed ten simultaneous editions in the English language!

D. L. Moody and R. A. Torrey were greatly helped by Finney's lectures, so that once again the fire of God fell.

The Promise of Revival

I often think, that young Evan Roberts, when still in his teens, must have pored over the writings of Charles Finney far into the night. The burden of revival weighed down the spirit of this young man, so that whenever he appeared before the Lord's people he wept and pleaded with them to prepare their hearts for the coming of the Holy Spirit. From the Welsh revival sprung many fires which burned simultaneously in different parts of the world.

One of the most moving calls to revival fell from the lips of A. T. Pierson as he ministered to the world's greatest evangelical congregation during the illness of its pastor, Charles Spurgeon:

> In this church there has been for months past one of the sublimest spectacles that has ever created joy in heaven, or in the midst of men. On the second Sunday of last May your beloved pastor was suddenly attacked with disease, and for twenty-one weeks daily prayer was offered for him in this Tabernacle, at early morning and evening. In these meetings the whole church of God seemed to be represented. All united in heart supplication to the living God to spare a life that they accounted of more value than the precious gold of Ophir, the onyx, or the sapphire. I say with pathos and deep persuasion that since the time the disciples waited ten days before God in continuous prayer for Pentecost, or

prayer was made "without ceasing" of the Church of God for Peter when in prison, there has been no spectacle so sublime presented by the Church of God during all these eighteen centuries! And now, in the Name of God, I challenge this great Church of Jesus Christ to a spectacle more sublime than that which has greeted the eyes of angels or men. *I want to challenge you—and this is the solemn conclusion of this solemn appeal—to an unceasing and united prayer for a new coming of the Holy Ghost on the Chinch and on the world.*

If this spectacle was sublime of all disciples of every name, uniting for the rescue of one beloved pastor from the jaws of death, how think you the heavenly hosts would thrill with delight, and even the heart of our Saviour, itself, if disciples of Jesus Christ of every name could be found represented in morning and evening meetings for prayer during six months to come, in this consecrated place, in an importunate, believing and anointed supplication that the greatest manifestation of the Holy Ghost since the ways of Pentecost might come upon the Church of God in this apostate age. And this, that the world might soon hear the tidings of the Gospel, that they might flash like electric lights from pole to pole, till every creature shall have learned the message of salvation, and that the Gospel shall have been preached as a witness to all nations, that the end might come, when the King in His glory shall once more descend to take His throne and wield His sceptre over the world.

Now, to our closing challenge of this book. To all who yearn for a deep spiritual awakening I would suggest that in every congregation a prayer circle be formed without regards to number. The pastor should unite with himself any members in whom he discerns a peculiar degree of spiritual life and power and, without any publicity, or any direct effort to enlarge such a company, begin with these to lay hold on God. The Holy Ghost, Himself, must add to the numbers and thus, quietly, and without observation, increase the little group under the blessing of the Lord. *It is essential that only prepared people, who are willing to pay the price for revival, join the prayer circle.*

It is also essential that these prayer meetings be not hurried. In my campaigns I often announce, "We are going to have a late prayer meeting. If you are nervous, or in a hurry to get home, kindly do not wait behind tonight, as the purpose of the meeting will be defeated, We want to have a quiet, unhurried waiting upon God." One must settle down in the Lord's presence before he can touch the Throne. It is in the stillness of the Holiest that the Father speaks. It is when we are quiet that the Holy Spirit prays through us. In order to have such definite prayer meetings for revival, Christians must be willing to sacrifice social pleasantries, and the comforts of life, including even sleep, and to lay aside everything that would hinder them in having these trysts with God.

Another point which I would like to emphasize is that no one should publicly pray in such gatherings until God has given him the spirit of faith; otherwise the prayer of faith will be severely weakened. I always tell the believers in large prayer meetings, "Kindly do not pray publicly until the Lord has given you the spirit of faith to believe that He is going to fulfil His Word." It is good sometimes for such believers to go aside together in mutual fellowship and cry to God until faith becomes their blessed portion. Faith grows upon the promises of God. Faith is grounded upon the Word of God. Thus it is necessary to study the Word and ask the Holy Spirit to seal it to your hearts. I have known on many occasions, when I was discouraged and downhearted, without any degree of faith that God would work in impossible situations, I was driven to the Book. After some hours in the Lord's presence, I got up from my knees with the Bible in my hands, singing:

> *High are the cities that dare our assault;*
> *Strong are the barriers that call us to halt!*
> *March we on fearless, and down they must fall,*
> *Vanquished by faith in Him—far above all"!*

It is important that general prayers be omitted in gatherings to pray for revival. Many meetings of such a nature are spoiled by some brother or sister praying general prayers "a round the world." Prayer, to be vital, must be definite. Ask the Holy

Ghost to pray through you in vital intercession for the one definite purpose of the reviving of a sub-normal church and the salvation of lost souls on their way to perdition.

When the prayer meetings grow, under the blessing of the Lord, and larger numbers gather, it is necessary then to pray more for the restraining and constraining power of the Holy Spirit. Many pastors are afraid to "throw open" the prayer meetings for united intercession because of the indefinite ramblings of some. One of the hardest things to acquire is the spirit of definite intercession. How few Christians will keep to the one theme of the meeting—revival! There is naturally a difference between a small group met together to pray and a large group—say of one thousand. In the small group the Holy Spirit sometimes burdens one believer to pray for half an hour, while in the large meeting this would be entirely out of place. When I have been conducting large prayer meetings I have asked the saints to make their prayers short and definite in order that a large number may take part. In a majority of cases four or five long prayers will kill the prayer meeting. In these large prayer meetings, where sometimes several thousands have gathered, we have found that the prayers which are most effective are those which range from three to five minutes. Of course, one must be careful not to set a rigid standard in such a meeting, as the Holy Spirit is sovereign in His working, and sometimes overthrows our schedule.

Many times we have found it very profitable in a local church for different age groups to meet in different rooms for prayer. This is exceedingly helpful as it gives opportunity for some timid souls to break forth in intercession at the Mercy

Seat. This helps to educate every soul in the assembly in the art of public prayer. It also gives more people an opportunity to take part.

It is preferable on many occasions for sisters to pray by themselves. In prayer meetings, when both sexes are present and the number is small, the conveners must be careful that at no time Satan be allowed an advantage. It is unwise, for instance, for sisters, whose unconverted husbands have remained at home, to meet for prayer with their brothers in the Lord whose unconverted wives are not present.

Every pastor, the moment he accepts the pastorate of a church, should seek at the earliest possible moment to establish a circle of prayer during the twenty-four hours of each day, when at all times some saint will be on the "watch tower" (Hab. 2:1). For over thirty years it has been our practice to carry on this twenty-four-hour chain of prayer in our meetings, with blessed results. I remember a church in Eastern Europe that built a special prayer tower, so that the members could carry on a cycle of prayer on the hour throughout the day and the night, as they looked down on the great needy city. In my whole life I never had such liberty in praying for any city as for that one. I seemed to understand with greater significance how Christ wept over Jerusalem.

It is good also for every church to set aside one or two definite rooms for intercession which may not be used for any other purpose. The setting apart of these rooms for the definite ministry of intercession somehow has a sobering effect upon the congregation.

The Promise of Revival

If your local church is really sincere in its prayer for revival, I would suggest that you gather in the following manner:

1. *Gather for prayer each Saturday night from eight o'clock till midnight.*

2. *On some week nights be prepared to pray as long as the Holy Spirit keeps you on your knees. Sometimes I have known that we missed a blessing from the Lord because some had not made preparation beforehand to remain longer.*

3. *On some occasions spend the entire night in prayer.*

4. *Each Lord's Day, gather for early morning prayer (the earlier the better, that the prayers will not be rushed) before the services of the day begin.*

5. *Have a prayer meeting prior to every Sunday evening Gospel service.* I have found that it is almost impossible to preach the Gospel with holy unction if there has not been a red-hot prayer meeting beforehand. I always feel sorry and depressed when I find a church which does not weep for souls, at least before the Gospel service. Believers who come to this evening service without having spent time alone with God for blessing only lend to the coldness of the atmosphere.

6. *Conduct a prayer meeting every week-day morning from 6-8 a.m.* This may seem impractical, owing to the different working hours of the various members of the assembly. However, if the church will persevere, they will find a practical solution for this early morning meeting. Some can only attend for fifteen

minutes before going to work, but we have known many churches to be revolutionized through the early morning prayer meeting.

Believers who cannot attend these early morning prayer meetings should seek to attend meetings for prayer at other hours, so that the cycle of prayer may be retained. For example, those who work on night shifts can attend meetings in the afternoons. Mothers and home-makers can attend either forenoon or afternoon meetings. Those who work down-town can pray during the lunch hour.

It is also necessary to conduct united prayer meetings, with all evangelical fundamental churches combining, from time to time. How tragic it is to see a city or nation with several evangelical groups, crying to God for the same blessing, who are not united in their plea. Dr. Dale said, in his day, that even the sunrise over Rigi in Switzerland was not so glorious as seeing the light of the Gospel break forth in all its majesty in the hearts and lives of the thousands who attended Moody's meetings in Britain. May I say that there is no sight so glorious here on earth as that of some four or five thousand believers gathered together night after night for united intercession.

Andrew Bonar said, "God loves unity, and so He loves a united cry; a petition signed by more than one."

In these united meetings different local pastors, or the spiritual leaders in their churches, should preside on different occasions to lend unity to the cause. On other occasions some outside Bible teacher or evangelist should be invited; men who know the deep mysterious workings of the Holy

Spirit in revival. At these meetings a short message should be given from the Word of God relating to prayer and victorious Christian living. Short expositions of the revivals under Ezra, Josiah, Hezekiah, and Nehemiah, etc., are helpful. In all revival praying our faith must be based on the Word of God alone. Any movement towards revival that neglects the Word of God is bound to end in mere excitement.

After relating how the revivals in the Bible were brought about, it is often very helpful to tell of the supernatural workings of God in the history of the Church. These revival times are a source of great encouragement to the believers. "Sweet are the spots where Emmanul has ever shown His glorious power in the conviction and conversion of sinners," said Samuel Rutherford.

One can understand the feelings of a Salvationist from the southern part of the U.S.A., on a pilgrimage to the city of London to visit the spot where William Booth commenced the work of the Salvation Army. After spending a hallowed time at Mile-End, he visited the Headquarters on Denmark Hill. There he gazed for a long time at the statue of the Founder. He was strangely moved. Reverently he knelt and sobbed out, "O Lord, do it again! O Lord, do it again!"

The father of William C. Burns, the minister at Kilsyth, encouraged himself in this same way. The subject of revival, as the great want of the times, had been for a long time in his mind and in the minds of the saints there. They could never forget what God did almost one hundred years before in the same parish. In to those sacred reminiscences and aspirations Mr. Burns entered most profoundly from the first day of his ministry in 1821. He laboured unceasing to keep alive, both in his own heart and the hearts of his people, the records of God's past dealings with His people. In 1822, the second year of his ministry, we find him, along with another congenial spirit, Dr. George Wright of Stirling, bending over the old records of the kirk-sessions, bearing on the dates 1742-9 and with solemn interest deciphering the dim and fading lines that referred to the incidents of the work then in progress. Towards the close of the same year, and two successful summers, he preached directly and fully on the subject, taking for his text those singularly appropriate and impressive words in Micah. 7:1, "Woe is me! for I am as when they have gathered the summer fruits, as the grapegleanings of the vintage: there is no cluster to eat; my soul desired the firstripe fruit," bringing the whole case of past attainment and subsequent declension before the people and calling upon them again to rise and seek the Lord.

Finally, on a Sunday afternoon, in August 1838, standing on the grave of his predecessor Mr. Robe on the anniversary of his death, he pleaded before a vast assembly of his people, in tones of unaccustomed earnestness which stirred the hearts of many in a manner never to be forgotten.

It was not very long after this that the heavens were rent and the whole parish was transformed like a garden of the Lord.

The pastor's son William, in like manner, reminded the believers of the "high days of God." It was while he was calling to mind the great achievements of the Spirit at the Kirk at Shotts, in 1630, under the preaching of John Livingstone, that the whole congregation at his father's church were overwhelmed with the mighty power of God. "The power of the Lord's Spirit became so mighty upon their souls as to carry all before it like the rushing mighty wind at Pentecost." At the same time, in the pulpit of Murray McCheyne at Dundee, he read as a part of the pulpit exercises, Robe's Monthly Narratives of the mighty movements of the Holy Spirit in Scotland and other lands. These accounts so raised the tide of faith of the believers at St. Peter's that very soon they were in the midst of revival themselves!

Let a record be kept of every definite petition laid before God. We must not mock God. It is necessary from time to time in these prayer meetings to stand up and tell how God has answered prayer in the salvation of loved ones and other deliverances.

It is essential from time to time to have solemn definite acts of dedication, for entire surrender is indispensable to the prayer of faith.

May God guide us in beginning *today* a full preparation for His gracious visitation among us in reviving power, "For great is the Holy One of Israel in the midst of thee" (Isa. 12:6).

www.ingramcontent.com/pod-product-compliance
Lightning Source LLC
Chambersburg PA
CBHW032019040426
42448CB00006B/674